POETSCAPES

POETSCAPES

Shruti Sharma

An Ink Gladiators Press® Publication

Ink Gladiators Press®
Publishing and promoting warriors on life's battlefield

Ink Gladiators Press is an ePublishing company whose mission is to publish and promote writers, poets, lyricists, artists and photographers through our current worldwide market distribution of over 3 billion readership. It is not affiliated with any other organization and is an independent ePublishing house. For Earthians who want to publish with us, check out our ongoing publishing opportunities at Our Earthians Community Group, or write to us to learn more about our high-end professional Celestial Sky Services at the following email address: contact@inkgladiatorspress.com

ISBN 13: 978-93-90766-50-5

Ink Gladiators Press®
Printed in Bangalore 560077, India
www.inkgladiatorspress.com

Credits:
Cover Photography – Shruti Sharma
Book Cover and Interior Design – Leonie Belle Hawk
Editor – Reena Doss

For everyone
who needs expression and refuge in words,
I hope my penned thoughts let you find them here.

Table Of Contents

I
Nano Poems

1. Poetscapes

I do love a little chaos
for poetry was never
a child of
order

2. Becoming the Bold

sit safely in comfort
or take that leap
the choice you make
makes the life you keep

3. Don't Give Up

when the winds blow harsh
like the end is near
just dig in those roots
and you will persevere

4. Old Eyes

and sometimes
I miss the wonder
in this one-click
world

5. On Memories

lovingly deceptive these waves
that come kiss your feet
then pull you under
as they retreat

6. Two-faced

and don't we all
chase the sun
while professing love
to the shade

7. Yearndays

days the heart yearns
for things
the mind cannot
identify

8. Rebel Sails

beauty in decay
defiance in her bones
she was a crumbling castle
staring down the ocean

9. Inevitable

not reserved for those in love
the pain of a broken heart
the wait is
its own heartbreak

10. Mr Wish

regret and I met once
early on in his career
we soon parted ways
our incompatibility clear

on far better terms am I
with a distant cousin of his
he visits once in a while
the whimsical Mr Wish

11. Nostalgia

scent of mango trees
on a summer breeze
carries tales of days
spent with skinned knees

12. Boundaries Required

we shoot from anger's bow
arrows tipped with pain
and the more we love someone
the more accurate our aim

II

Short Poems

1. A Season for All

next time you feel
too old, too late
I hope that you remember
Summer's kiss comes
to some in May
to others in December

2. Unchain me

if only for a few hours
truly unbound
not by anyone, not by anything
I can't be found
all that weighs me down
left in gravity's ground

I'm sky-bound

3. The Right Decision

she changed her path
the day she started
extending her Sundays
to avoid her Mondays

days should be lived
not feared

4. Take it in

learn to be still
you are a passenger
on time's train
alight at stations
once in a while
or your weary soul
will not sustain

5. Autumn Musings

burnished leaves dancing
a kaleidoscopic ballet
at my feet find
their resting place
as I pick one to marvel
at its beautiful death
it finds the sun
and shows me
the flaming life within

6. Ongoing Battle

glittering in reach
this mirage of security
beckoning bright through
the lens of reason
but my whimsical heart
from these moorings must part
for the dreamer in me
 is playing treason

7. Your Story

we all have one
crafted over time
by laughter lightened
by tears lined
by hate pounded
by love caressed
by years layered
by memories dressed
so unveil yours for me
in all its weathered glory
tell me who you are
tell me, what's your story?

8. Black and White

I open yellowed albums
of childhood chronicles
rainbow of moments
painted black and white

a perfect pairing
memories and monochrome
nostalgia speaks loudest
when not drowned by noisy colours

9. Exchanging Roles

I see your 'I feel invisible'
and raise you 'I wish I was'
and were pain comparable
I'd wonder which one
a deeper heartache does cause

10. I Think of You

I think of you
just a little these days

a little more often than I should
a little less guarded than I could
as each day dawns a little less bright
you feel to me a little more right
each moment we grow a little less apart
time's false hope a little more stark
and as I sit hitting keys to your tune
I'm a little less found
a little more lost

yes, I think of you
just a little these days

11. Portrait of an Extrovert

you are the fathomless blue
sparking aqua off the sun
many bask in your warm surface
follow the rays down do a few
then those secret trenches
where dwell creatures so wildly bright
you shield them from the light

12. Dream Strong

fragile dreams
birth secret needs
that resentment feed
but have not the will
to succeed

13. Larger than Life

warm heart
kaleidoscopic smile
burnished spirit
of fiery hues
amber words rustle
tinted silver
crisp tone
still make me quiver
a fearless Fall
marching towards Winter
my Mother

14. Inner Goals

the crystal shone
diamond bright
flashed the same fire
yet lost the fight
and I wonder why
these diamonds we desire
is it their beauty
or their price that is higher

15. The World's Race

run, push, climb higher
scrambling ticking hearts
unquenchable thirst of desire
bury, drown, extinguish
unheard knocking and tocking souls
pulses marking sad time
to the metronomes
of earthly goals

16. My One and Only Hero

I remember days ending
in piggyback rides and fairytales
when being tossed high
didn't come attached
with the fear of the fall
when I knew it really would be okay
I had a superhero on call
fondest of memories
those days when
my father's shoulders
carried my worries
as easily as they did
my weight

17. Cliff Notes

I stand on the edge
of this ocean ledge
and wonder how many
whispered sighs it has heard

salty tears rest easy
on creased cheeks
they feel at home here
with the breeze

waves echo the beat
of crashing hearts
the bruised ones
and those torn apart

as the sun bleeds
in hues of pain
the horizon paints
heartache's refrain

in unfailing return
the tides show
all of this life
is ebb and flow

18. Nature's Sounds

I sat in the courtyard
lost in the happy intersection
of whispering leaves
gossiping birds
and absent footsteps
and then rang the temple bell
making the silence shatter
the birds scatter
and me wonder…
why is it that all of Nature's sounds soothe
while ours disturb?

19. Alone

so you kept feeding
pieces of you to that fire
of their needs
of their desires

you forgot fuel's fate
to burn, to be consumed

and ever so lovely be that heat
ever so bright that light
it's not your hands
it'll warm, love
on a cold Winter's night

20. Hard Truths

so lost in being the hero
in everyone else's story
you never realized
when you became
the villain of your own

21. Caged In

we build our house of normal
with bricks of conformity
put a lock of obedience
and hide the key under
the mat of fear

22. Girls Like You

look at that hemline
just skimming your thighs
girls like you
shouldn't ask why

at 2 in the night
you were out and high
girls like you
don't get to cry

he's your husband
and you said no?
girls like you
should let it go

and I wonder how
it came about
'girls like you'
drowned girls out

23. Impenetrable

don't go building
those walls so high
your eyes forget
how blue the sky

a heart kept safe
in isolation's domain
forgets how to feel
and not just the pain

24. Under the Surface

you can have
the appearance of everything
and still your soul by sorrow gloved

if a book be well dusted
does it follow that
it is well loved?

25. Strange Facts

funny how the winds of success
were the ones to rock our boat
when the storms of failure
taught it how to float

who knew we'd win the war
just to go down in a fight
something went wrong
when everything went right

26. Unappreciative

grudging praise
half-hearted apologies
reluctant credit
rationed time

how selfish you got while giving
what you love receiving

27. My Space

there is a sanctuary
of words I escape to
of sparkling shadows
and winged feet

where perception and reality
dance a teasing waltz
and I can never tell
which one is leading

28. Comfort

I know it feels like
someone turned the lights off
and you're stumbling around
in unending darkness

but trust me when I say
one day the switch will flip
it takes but an instant
for light to breach dark

until then, darling,
when the demons come calling
let them meet the girl who sings yesterday
so sweetly in the today

loving hands will catch
should you fall
loving hearts will hear
when you call

29. What If I…

what if I walked into the storm…

would lightning strike down
or recharge
would the winds toss around
or elevate
would the rain drown
or rejuvenate

what if I walked into the storm
I've been running from?

30. Distorted Sight

I'm not certain
when a mirror's purpose
became to find fault
when the rushing breeze
through my hair became
an unwelcome touch
I recall a time
when the former made me laugh
and the latter felt right
I recall a time when
happiness was not a trophy
for which you had to fight

31. Summer's Reflections

the dwindling day's gentle rays
dapple through filigreed trees
they dance on my upturned face
my skirt flirts with the cool breeze

absent footsteps heighten
solitude's reflective state
I walk barefoot on the grass
the earth dictates my gait

in a quiet corner of the garden
luminous white petals sway
their beauty wraps arounds me
it is a perfect Summer's day

III

Form Poems

1. Lost Childhood
(an A-Z poem)

a boy ceding dreams
exchanged for guns
hate injected juggernaut
killing love mercilessly
narrowly oppressing pain
quoting rage seamlessly
this unloved, valiant
warmongering xeroxed
young zealot

2. Unprepared
(a Diminishing poem)

I was not supposed to feel this much pain, right?

I was not supposed to feel this much pain

I was not supposed to feel this much

I was not supposed to feel this

I was not supposed to feel

I was not supposed to

I was not supposed

I was not

I was

I

3. Famine Relief
(a Tanka poem)

earth struck by Sun's whip

beaten into submission

parched heart bubbling heat

yet in rain's healing caress

finding its petrichor beat

4. Depression
(a Reversible poem)

leave me alone

please don't

insist on staying

as I fall apart

as my sanity departs

walk away

don't you dare

stay

5. Another Year
(an Elfchen poem)

October
senses hone
into time's metronome
presents, reflection, inevitable introspection
birthday

6. Heart of a Child
(a Haiku poem)

butterfly flutters by

legs itch to chase and capture

rainbows and rapture

7. Instructions to Fly
(an Octelle poem)

don't go down that slide of dismay

let's try to swing this pain away

gentle push is all you need

off the ground, now build that speed

you're so high, the sky is low

close your eyes and let it go

don't go down that slide of dismay

let's try to swing this pain away

About The Author

Shruti Sharma is an introverted extrovert with a passion for all things related to travel. She prefers mountains over all other landscapes and dogs over all other animals. Her idea of a great time is to get lost in a good book, Mother Nature or with a good book in the lap of Mother Nature.

Apart from her passion for photography, writing and all things blue, she loves hanging out with her family and good friends. Having left her long-time corporate job, she is currently exploring things that make her happy, publishing her work in anthologies and hoping to find her life's purpose.

She recently published her debut photography book—*Monsoon Tales: through the lens of my 9th floor in Bangalore*—with Ink Gladiators Press and is looking forward to releasing more publications in the future.

Poetscapes | Shrutiscapes | Facebook | Goodreads | Amazon
www.shrutiscapes.com

Please scan the following QR code to follow Shruti Sharma.

Tell Us What You Think

Write to us at contact@inkgladiatorspress.com. We might add your comments or reviews on our website as well as feature your Instagram profile. We appreciate your love for reading.

Thank you!
We remain at your service,
Reena Doss | Founder
Ink Gladiators Press®

Please scan the following QR code to follow IGP.

www.ingramcontent.com/pod-product-compliance
Lightning Source LLC
Chambersburg PA
CBHW070317160726
47999CB00003B/1063